S of America

LITTLE ROCK

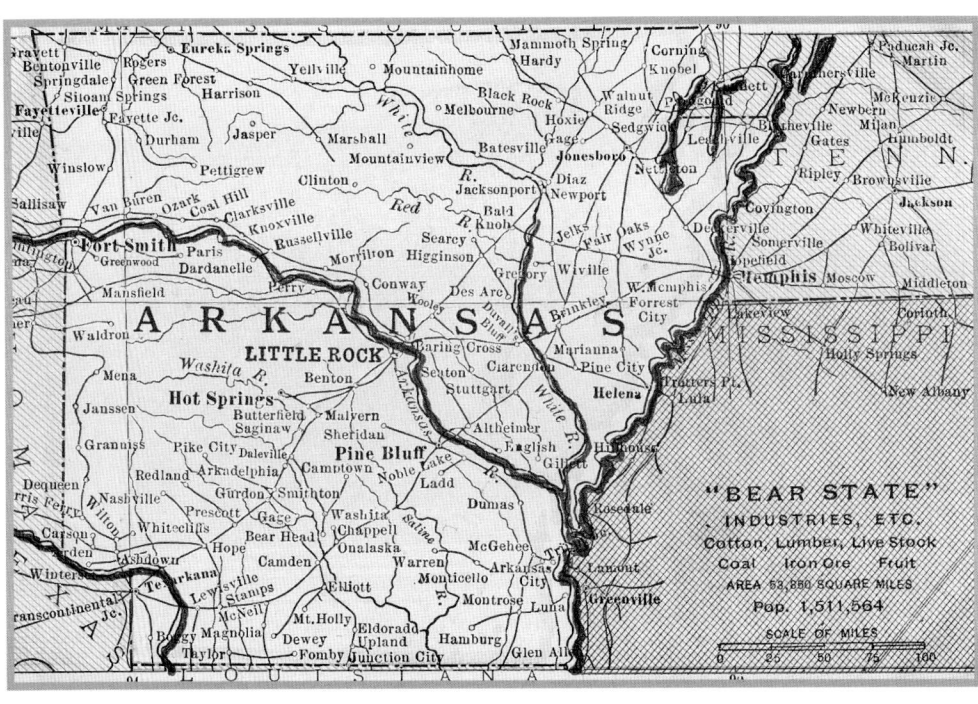

SCENES of America
LITTLE ROCK

**STEVEN G. HANLEY
AND RAY HANLEY**

Copyright © 2005 by Steven G. Hanley and Ray Hanley
ISBN 0-7385-2478-6

Published by Arcadia Publishing
Charleston SC, Chicago IL, Portsmouth NH, San Francisco CA

Library of Congress control number: 2005938139

For all general information contact Arcadia Publishing at:
Telephone 843-853-2070
Fax 843-853-0044
E-mail sales@arcadiapublishing.com
For customer service and orders:
Toll-Free 1-888-313-2665

Visit us on the internet at www.arcadiapublishing.com

*To our friend
Laura Alice Henson (1919–1996)
a lifelong resident of Little Rock.*

Special thanks to Audrey Burtrum-Stanley, Curtis Sykes, and John Cook,
for special input on North Little Rock.
Appreciation is given to Peg Smith, Jim Pfeifer,
Jim Eison, and Tom Mertens of Little Rock
for loaning their postcards
and for providing us access to their store of knowledge about our community.
Very special appreciation is extended to Diane Hanley,
for endless hours of editing, patience, and invaluable advice.

INTRODUCTION

French explorer Bernard de LaHarpe journeyed up the Arkansas River in May 1722 in search of what Native Americans described as a "giant green rock." LaHarpe hoped it might turn out to be a huge emerald. He found no precious stones, but he did find a large rock outcropping on the north side of the river and a smaller one on the south bank christened "La Petite Roche"—The Little Rock.

Because it was a convenient fording place, the landmark became an important crossroads in the nation's westward movement. The Southwest Trail, the busiest route between St. Louis and Texas, crossed the Arkansas River here. A rugged frontier settlement grew up at the ford. In March 1820, a post office was established with the official name "Little Rock," and Amos Wheeler was appointed postmaster. The town boasted only 12 to 15 white residents, all male, and one frame building surrounded by three or four log cabins.

Postmaster Wheeler submitted a proposal to the new Arkansas Territorial Legislature to move the capital from the malaria-ridden bottom lands of Arkansas Post in southeastern Arkansas to the healthier elevated location of Little Rock. Wheeler included an offer to donate land for a public square if the move were made. In October 1821, Little Rock became the territorial capital.

Arkansas was admitted to the Union on June 15, 1836, as the 25th state. The following September, the state legislature met in the new State House on Markham Street. During this first session, the lawmakers authorized the purchase of 36 acres within the city for construction of a federal arsenal. Forty-four years later, in 1880, World War II hero Gen. Douglas MacArthur was born on this post. Today the site is a city park named in his honor.

By 1900, Little Rock's population had grown to 38,307 residents, most of whom lived in houses built since the Civil War; the city was poised for a period of great economic growth. Its thriving business district boasted a seven-story commercial building, the tallest in the state, and ground was being broken on the far western edge of the city for a new state capital building. Indeed, Little Rock was on the brink of a period of tremendous growth, and photography would be there to capture the images of the early century that had dawned so brightly.

While the people of Little Rock may have changed little, the landscape itself has undergone profound changes. From the progress of Main Street, the rise and fall of passenger railroads, travel by river, and the building of churches and homes, nowhere are these changes more evident than in the comparison of what we see and do in our 21st-century lives with the images found in this book—images that trace the evolution of American life.

Little Rock is rich in history, and we are indeed fortunate that so much of it was recorded in photographs like the ones found in this book.

The capital city's namesake "little rock," discovered by French explorer Bernard de LaHarpe in 1722, became the subject of a popular postcard. The landmark was partially destroyed during the construction of the railroad bridge shown on this 1905 card. For much of the 20th century the rock was obscured by weeds and neglect. It was cleaned up and marked as a part of the city's riverfront redevelopment in the 1980s.

In 1936, the centennial year of Arkansas's statehood, one of its important territorial era buildings stood grossly neglected. This building at Third and Cumberland Streets, with Coca-Cola and Falstaff Beer signs nailed to its warped siding, was erected in 1828 by the family of Jesse Hinderliter to serve both as their home and as a tavern. The historic building was saved by Mrs. J. H. Loughborough, wife of a prominent local attorney, who persuaded the Arkansas Legislature to purchase the property for restoration. Today the restored building is a part of the Arkansas Territorial Restoration.

Four years after statehood, Arkansas had its first state capitol, known today as the Old State House. Building began in 1833 and was not declared complete until 1842. The Greek Revival building faced the city's main thoroughfare, Markham Street, with the Arkansas River offering a sweeping view of steamboats and the still wild north side of the river. The building was not without its critics; eccentric poet Albert Pike said it was "a great, awkward, clumsy, heavy edifice." When this c. 1900 view was taken, the cornerstone had been laid for the modern-day capitol, and the future fate of the state house was uncertain. Fortunately, the structure was saved and has become one of the city's best-known landmarks.

Markham and Main Streets, looking East on Markham, Little Rock, Ark. 1864, showing the Anthony House.

"Little Rock is quite historic. It dates back a century. The *Arkansas Gazette*, with which I did business, is 94 years old." These words were written on this c. 1913 postcard of a painting showing an 1864 view of the heart of the capital city, which was then occupied by the Union Army. The three-story building was the Anthony Hotel, built in 1840 and burned in 1875. Today the site is occupied by the Little Rock Convention Center.

The School for Deaf Children was established at Little Rock in 1867 by Joseph Mount, a deaf man who trained at the Pennsylvania Institute for the Deaf. The State of Arkansas took over the facility in 1868 and at the turn of the century built this imposing central building on West Markham Street. The school still serves children today, but in more modern buildings on the original campus. (c. 1910.)

The state-funded Confederate Soldiers' Home, before which a line of grizzled veterans posed, was located in the Sweet Home community east of Little Rock. In 1890, the war had been over for 25 years, and the need to care for the aging veterans began to weigh on the conscience of the state's citizens. With a legislative appropriation, the building seen on this card was erected in 1892 and became a new state institution. The home was bulldozed in 1943 because the nation's effort to win World War II required access to the bauxite deposits beneath the grand old building. The remaining 82 residents—only four of whom were veterans, the rest mostly widows—were relocated to the campus of the state's School for the Blind. According to the *Arkansas Democrat*, "None are more willing than the boys in gray and their women folk to make, just as they did almost a century ago, whatever sacrifice seems necessary to meet the their country's needs."

Riverboats of all types and sizes were a vital part of commerce on the often treacherous Arkansas River, in part because of its connection with the mighty Mississippi in the southeastern part of the state. The riverboat *Choctaw* transported cotton, livestock feed, and other goods, while a few passengers and crew could be housed on its second level. The arrival of the more reliable railroads in the late 19th century greatly diminished the importance of the riverboats. (c. 1900.)

The Pulaski County Courthouse was erected at Second and Spring Streets between 1887 and 1889 at a cost of $100,000. The building was constructed of blue granite taken from the Fourche Mountain Quarry east of Little Rock and was enhanced by terra cotta trim and distinctive gables. The top of the tower was removed in 1961 because of concerns about its structural integrity. The entire building was restored in the 1990s. (c. 1900.)

OPPOSITE: This is a 1917 view of the annex to the Pulaski County Courthouse, which was completed in 1914 from a design by noted architect George Mann, who also designed the new state capitol. The end result was a beautiful building that still serves today.

The Kempner Theater, named for a prominent Jewish family that immigrated to Little Rock in the 19th century, was located in the 600 block of Center Street. While other local theaters favored silent films, the Kempner was partial to lectures and plays. The Kempner later became a movie theater and was renamed the Arkansas Theater. It was active during the 1960s and 1970s, and then stood boarded in decay for a decade before being razed in 1997 for a parking lot. (c. 1900.)

Looking north from the 400 block of Main, the photographer captured the street before automobiles took over. Streetcars, initially pulled by mules, had come to Little Rock in 1877 and would be fixtures until replaced by buses in 1947. Among the businesses seen here are names from retailing history such as Pfeifer's and the Gus Blass Dry Goods establishment, seen on the left. (c. 1905.)

The Free Bridge was designed for foot and wagon traffic when it was erected in 1897. The wide path along the rails provided ample space to separate pedestrians from horses and wagons. The bridge ran from the foot of Main Street in Little Rock to Maple Street on the north side of the river. (c. 1905.)

The First Presbyterian Church, founded in 1828, may be the oldest continuously functioning church in the city today. The building shown in this 1908 photograph was built in 1868 at the corner of Fifth and Scott Streets, the first church erected after the Civil War. On the left is the back of the Masonic Temple. A newer building serves at a different location and this site is now a parking lot.

OPPOSITE: This 1905 view from atop the Hotel Marion looks over the Capital Hotel toward the Masonic Temple and Catholic Cathedral. The spire to the left is Christ Episcopal.

The Missouri Pacific–Iron Mountain Railroad erected this impressive station in 1911 on Victory Street, in prominent view of the new state capitol building. This c. 1912 postcard published by the railroad boasted that the station was "one of the handsomest and most conveniently arranged railroad stations in America. No state in the Union surpasses Arkansas in natural resources. In this great state Missouri Pacific–Iron Mountain has a total mileage of almost 2,400 miles or almost ten times the extreme length of the state. Its lines reach out in all directions from Little Rock. Forty-two Missouri Pacific passenger trains arrive at and depart from Little Rock daily. Little Rock is the shortest route between St. Louis, Texas, and Mexico." The number of daily passenger trains mentioned clearly reflects the major role railroads played in Little Rock at the time. The station burned in 1922 but was quickly rebuilt.

Under construction at the time this photograph was taken in 1906, the rising tower of the Union Station afforded this view up Markham street looking toward downtown. Visible in the distance is the clock tower of the Pulaski County Court House.

The Blind School's commanding presence at the intersection of Eighteenth and Center Streets is clearly evident from this 1908 postcard. The street leading up to the school was lined with large homes that still stand today. The school, however, was relocated to its present location on West Markham in 1939, and the towered building was torn down in 1948 to make way for the construction of the new governor's mansion.

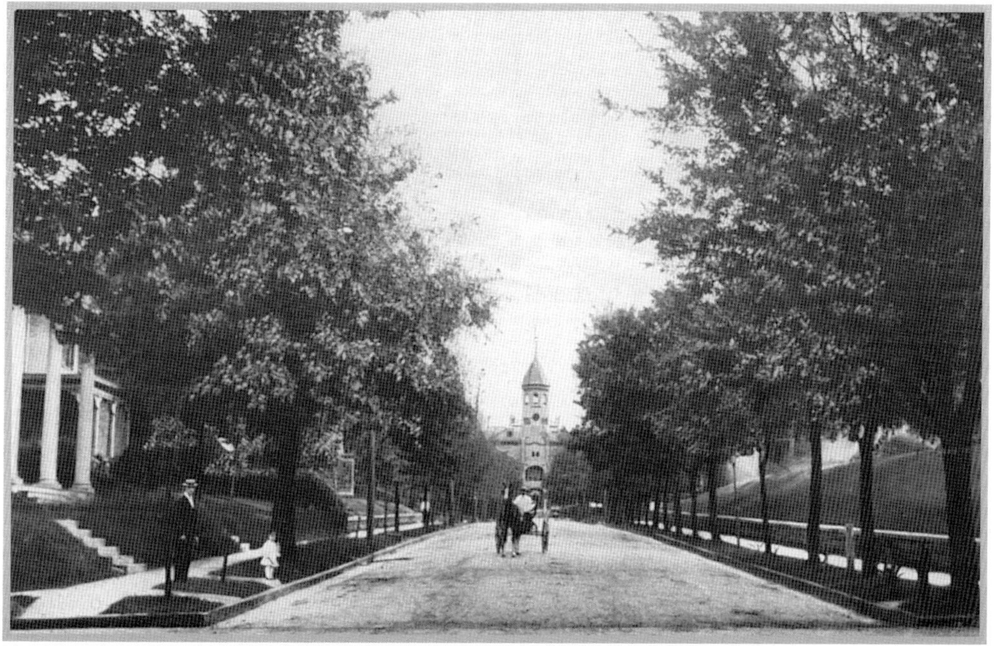

Little Rock High School was built at the turn of the 20th century, at the corner of Fourteenth and Scott Streets. The school served as the city's high school for white students until the opening of Central High School in 1927. The 1908 boys' football team posed here with what seems to have been a mascot bulldog.

OPPOSITE: In later years, Little Rock High School served various other purposes, including use as an adult vocational school. The building has now been restored and remains in use. (c. 1910.)

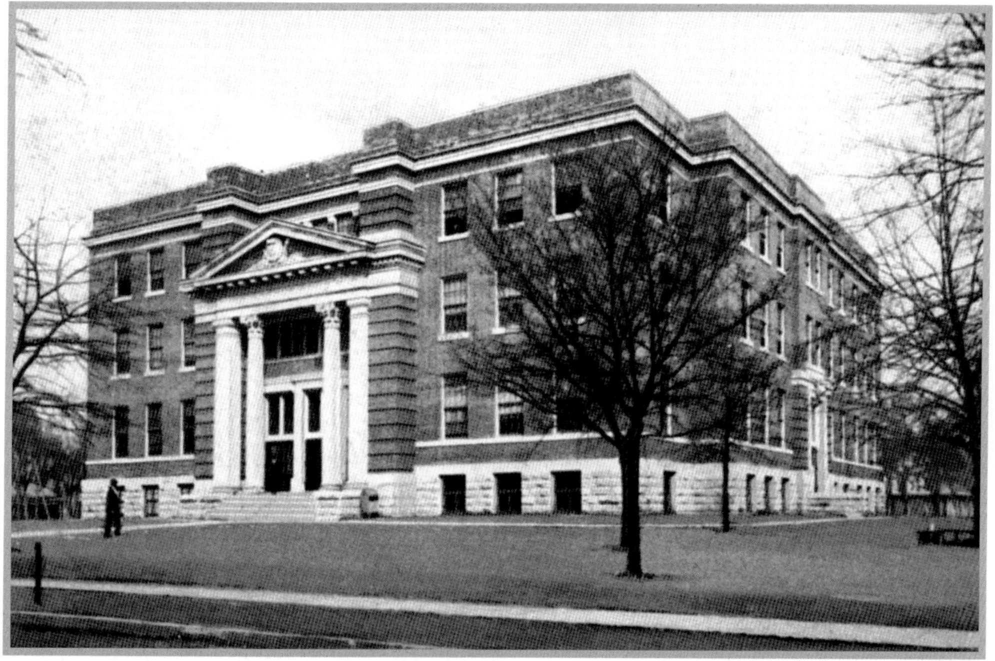

The Fred Kramer School, shown c. 1908, was erected in 1895 on Sherman Street between Seventh and Eighth Streets. Its distinctive tower was removed some 50 years later, and the building sat boarded and decaying for much of the 1980s and 1990s. This oldest surviving public school building in Little Rock was saved and restored as a resident artists' gallery in 1997.

OPPOSITE: The William Woodruff School held an "Open air school" in 1911 under this large tent. Named for the founder of the *Arkansas Gazette*, the school still stands on West Seventh Street and continues to educate the children of Little Rock as Woodruff Elementary.

43

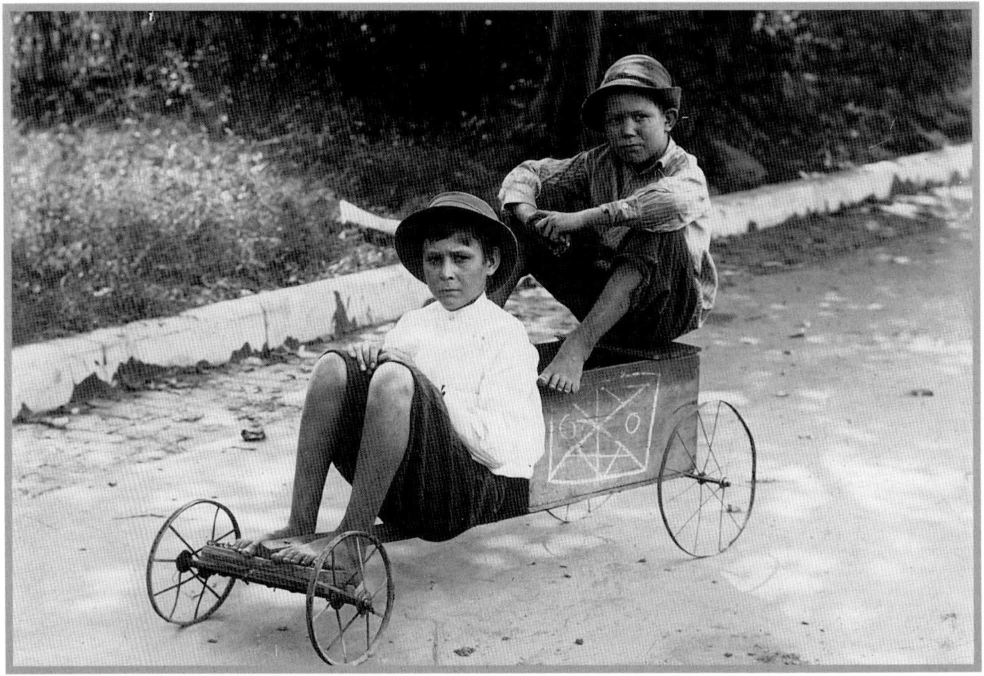

The street in front of the Kennedy home at 1221 West Sixth Street was the testing ground for brothers Norman and Robert's homemade car. These children, who lived in a working-class neighborhood, were shoeless but had their hats on, ready to ride a vehicle with few safety features. (c. 1908.)

Boulevard Park, later renamed Braddock's Park, was a private park built in part to boost business for the streetcar company. The park's "Wonderland" amusement area, the entrance of which is seen to the right of the streetcar in this c. 1905 view, ran from Thirty-sixth Street southwest to the Choctaw (later Rock Island) railroad tracks, near today's state fair grounds. The area is reserved as a park today. In this view, the two conductors had stopped their car where the tracks ended at the park gate.

ROCK ISLAND DEPOT
PLEASE PAY CONDUCTOR ON ENTERING CAR
218
WOND

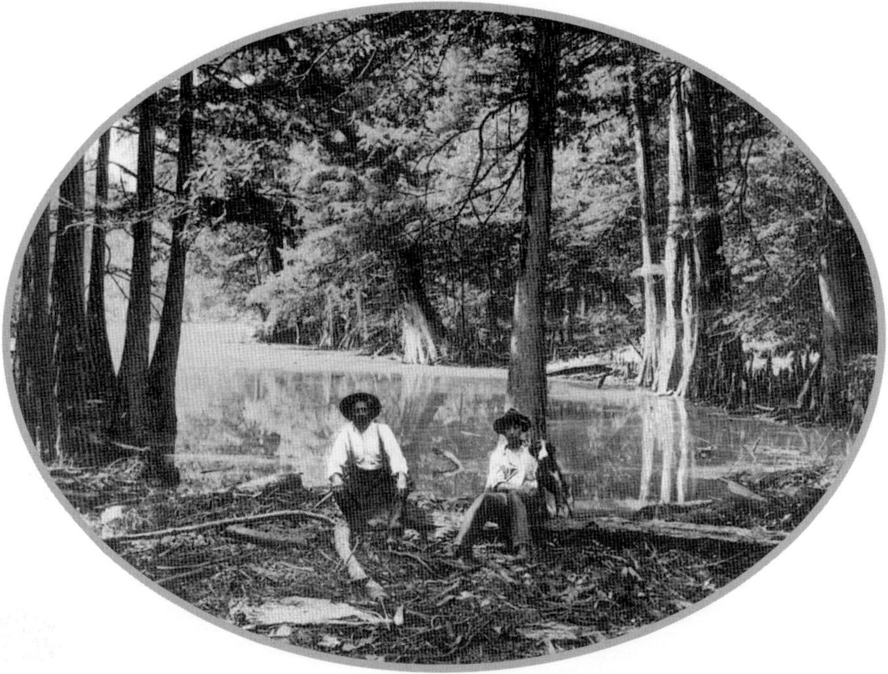

Little Rock in the early 20th century was bounded on the east and south by vast wetlands of huge cypress trees and the bottomland swamps of Fourche Creek. These wild areas survived for many years in part due to the difficulty of extracting the timber. In early days the wetlands provided a sportsman's refuge near the city. A father and son and their dog posed in a cypress brake for this *c.* 1908 photograph.

The University of Arkansas School of Medicine, located near City Park, educated most of the physicians who would serve the expanding hospital systems of Little Rock. This group of medical students posed with a skeleton and the physician's traditional black bag in 1908.

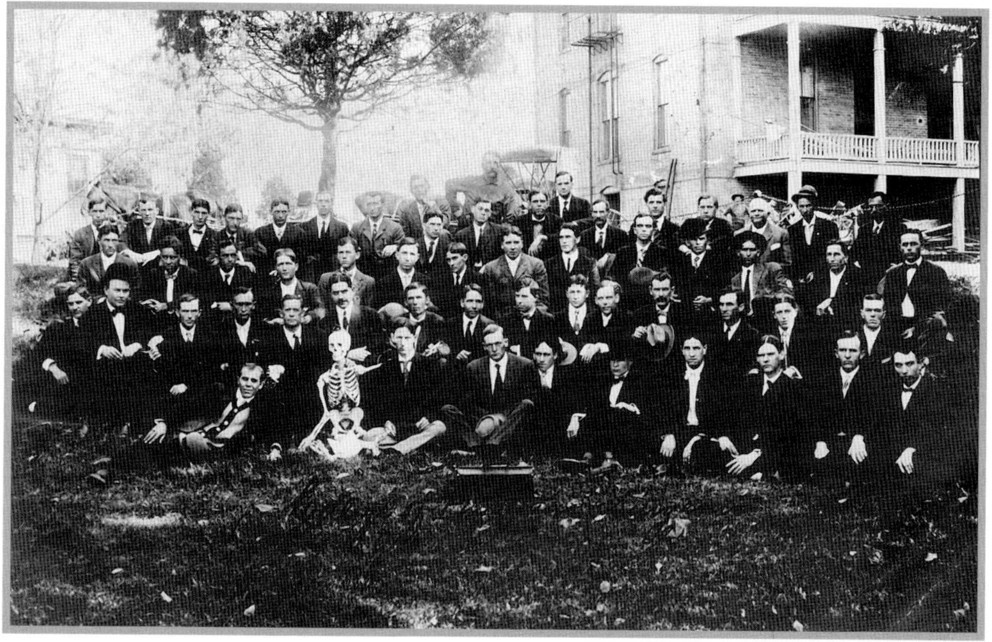

AMERICAN TOUR 1908-9

MYRTLE ELVYN, PIANISTE

Recital

THURSDAY EVENING, FEBRUARY 27, 1908
CAPITAL THEATER
LITTLE ROCK, ARK.

PROGRAM

1. (a) PRELUDE AND FUGUE, A MINOR . . . BACH
   (TRANSCRIBED FROM THE ORGAN BY LISZT)
   (b) SONATA APPASSIONATA, OP. 57 . BEETHOVEN
   ALLEGRO ASSAI—ANDANTE CON MOTO
   ALLEGRO MA NON TROPPO

2. (a) POSTORALE (ANGELUS) . CORELLI (1653-1713)
   (b) TAMBOURIN . . . . RAMEAU (1683-1764)
   (NEWLY ARRANGED BY LEOPOLD GODOWSKY)
   (c) RHAPSODIE, B MINOR, OP 79 . . BRAHMS

3. (a) NOCTURNE, G MAJOR, OP. 37 } CHOPIN
   (b) POLONAISE, A FLAT MAJOR, OP. 53

4. (a) RHAPSODIE NO. 12 . . . . LISZT
   (b) BERCEUSE . . . . HENSELT
   (c) ARABESQUES ON STRAUSS' WALZER, "ON
   THE BEAUTIFUL BLUE DANUBE" . SCHULZ-EVLER
   (NEWLY ARRANGED BY LEOPOLD GODOWSKY)

KIMBALL PIANO USED

Touring performers like pianist Myrtle Elvyn often filled theaters' open times between screenings of early silent films. According to this ad, Elvyn gave a recital in Little Rock on Thursday evening, February 27, 1908.

This large house with multiple fireplaces was one of a line of similar new homes erected together, seen here stretching down the 2300 block of Battery Street in 1909. Today these homes still stand amidst tall trees, though some are in a state of disrepair brought on by the shift of the city's population to distant suburbs.

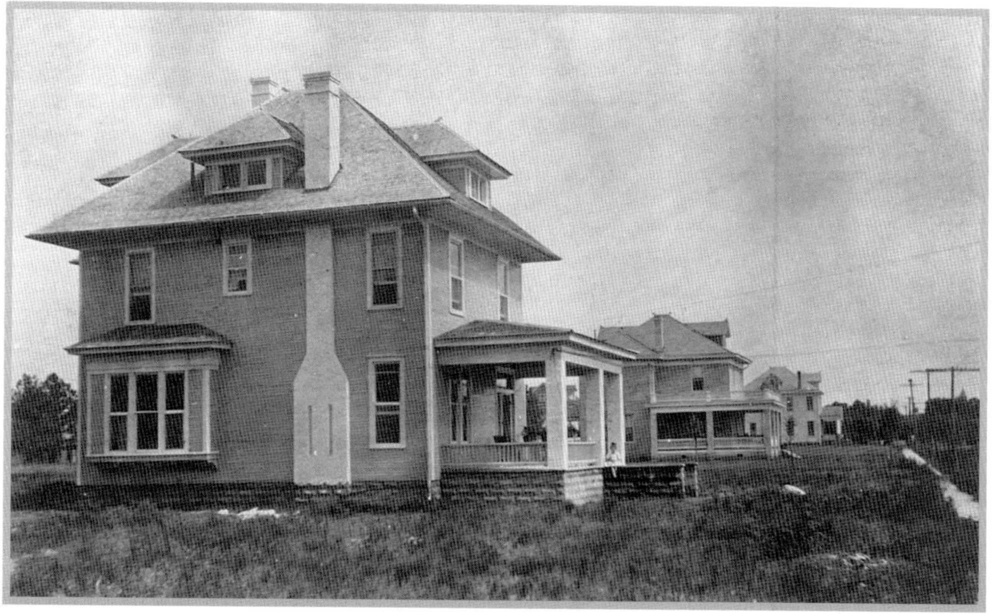

56

The new state capitol was nearing completion in 1910, though construction had been delayed for several years by inefficiency and a bribery scandal. The legislature first met in the partially completed building in 1911. The *Arkansas Gazette* summed up the state's pride in the new building when it declared, "The Capitol Commission's gift to the state of Arkansas in 1910 will be the magnificent new State Capitol that stands like the Parthenon of old on the eminence of the western extremity of the Fifth Street."

A photographer climbed to the dome of the new capitol building and pointed his camera east down Capitol Avenue toward distant Main Street to capture this c. 1910 view of the city. The wide boulevard of Capitol Avenue was traversed by streetcars and a few wagons that moved past large homes, all of which are gone today.

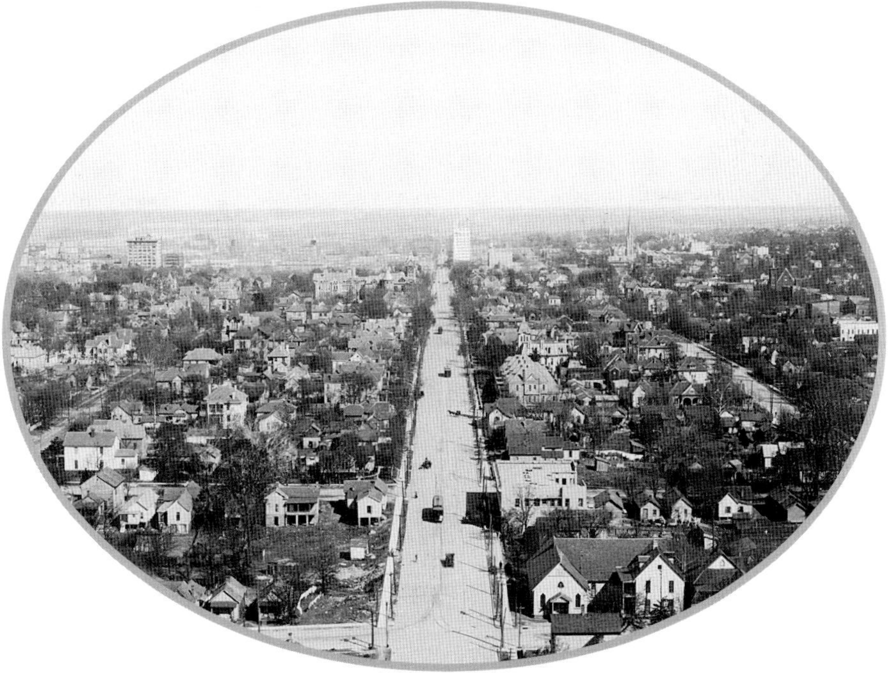

MAIN ST. SOUTH FROM SECOND ST.

The new electric streetlights were on in this unusual 1910 nighttime postcard. The view looks south down the east side of Main Street. Such technological improvements were signs of the first-class city Little Rock was becoming in the early years of the 20th century.

This train steaming south would have been only minutes out of the Union Station, as it passed the area known as Lincoln Avenue Hill near what is presently called Cantrell Road. The area was also known locally at that time as "Carpetbagger Row" because of the mansions built by wealthy northerners who came to the city during the Reconstruction period following the Civil War. The twin spires in the background belonged to the Physicians and Surgeons Hospital. (c. 1910.)

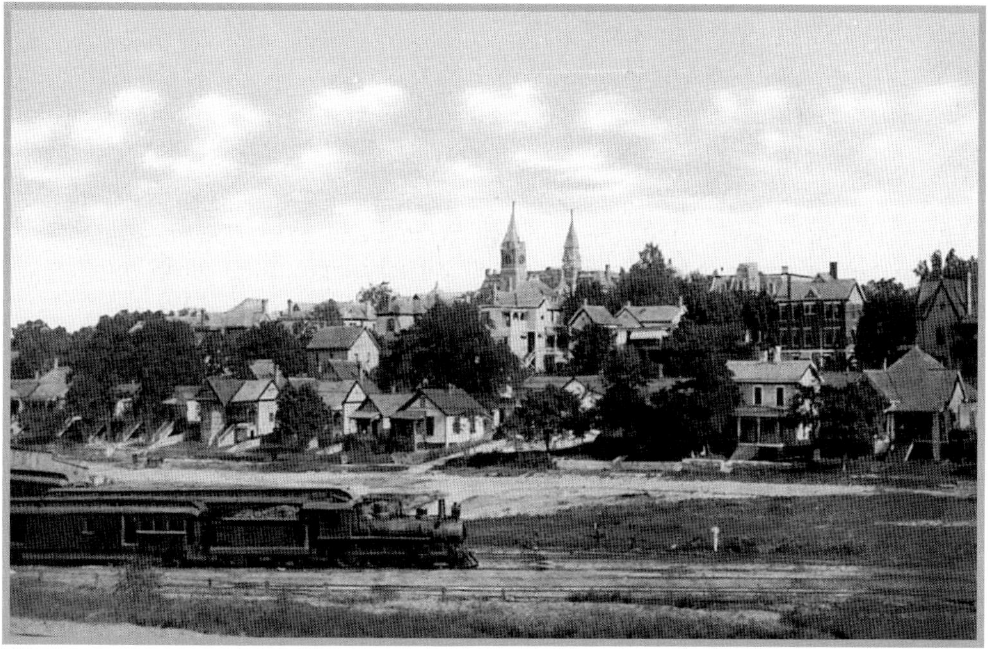

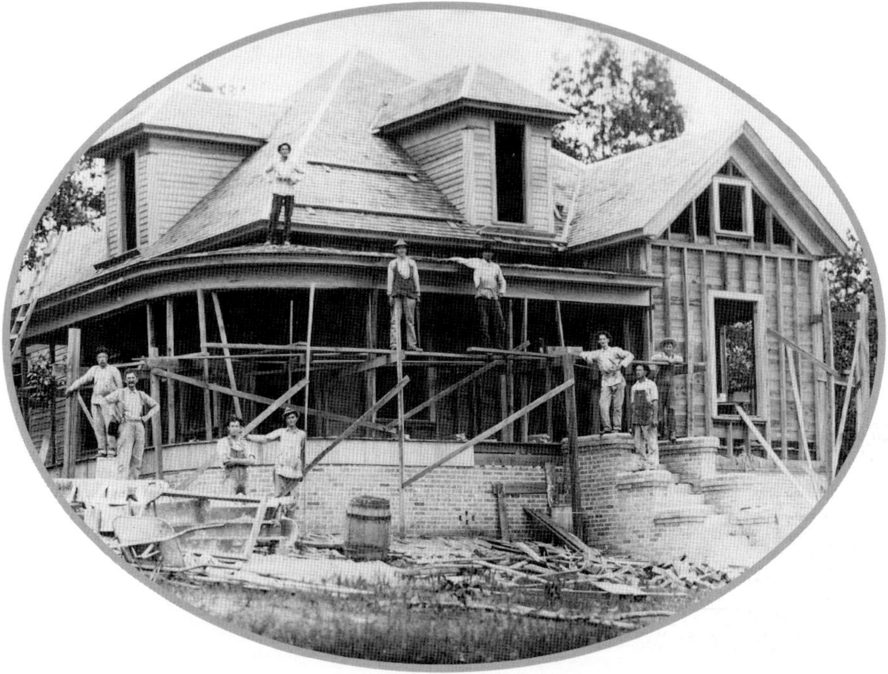

This relatively modest Little Rock home was photographed during its construction at 1424 West Fourth Street c. 1910. The labor-intensive nature of construction in the era before power tools is illustrated by the 10 workers pictured in this scene. The house was demolished in the 1960s.

Led by Little Rock businessman Horace Pugh, a group of concerned citizens founded the Arkansas Children's Home in 1912. In an effort to provide much needed medical care to youngsters, Superintendent Orlando P. Christian, a retired Methodist minister, added a hospital in 1926. The orphanage closed in 1954, but the Arkansas Children's Hospital has grown to become one of America's leading pediatric medical centers.

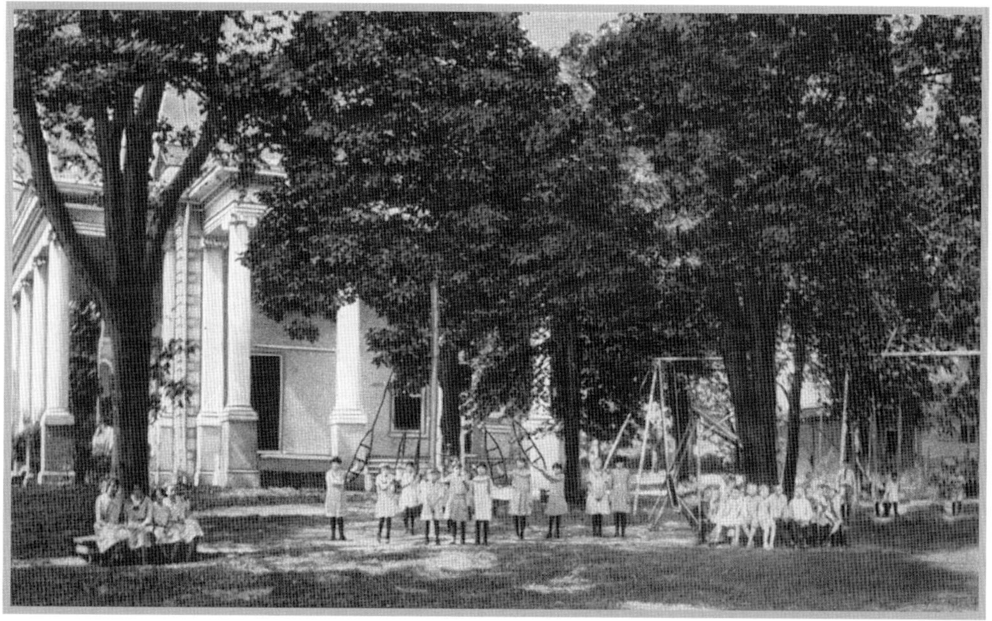

FOR SALE HERE
VARIETY
HARPERS
LESLIES
Collier's
Collier's
VARIETY
GREEN BOOK

The bustling Rock Island Station rail depot housed this newsstand to serve travelers. Among the magazines were *Collier's*, *Variety*, and *Harpers Weekly*, in addition to a well-stocked postcard rack to the right and a variety of souvenirs, books, and other items. Today the building is part of the Presidential Library and Museum complex showcasing President Bill Clinton's White House years. Ironically, the issue of *Leslie's* on display in the upper left features a cover story entitled "Presidential Valentines."

Sports has always played a part in the education of the young women attending Mount Saint Mary's. In this *c.* 1910 photograph, the supervising nuns keep a watchful eye on the dirt basketball court.

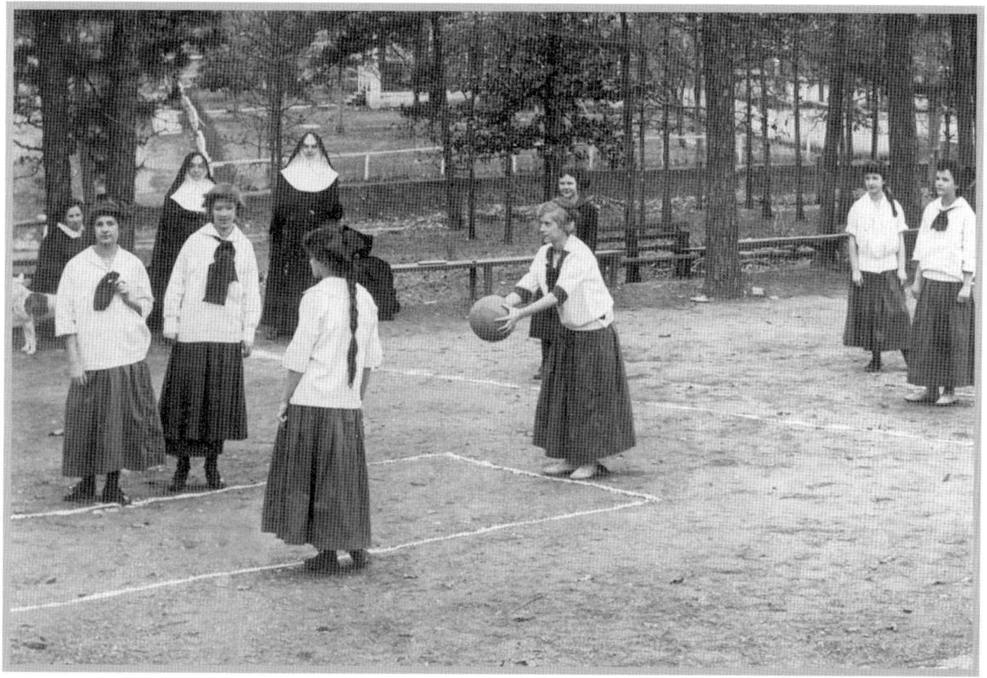

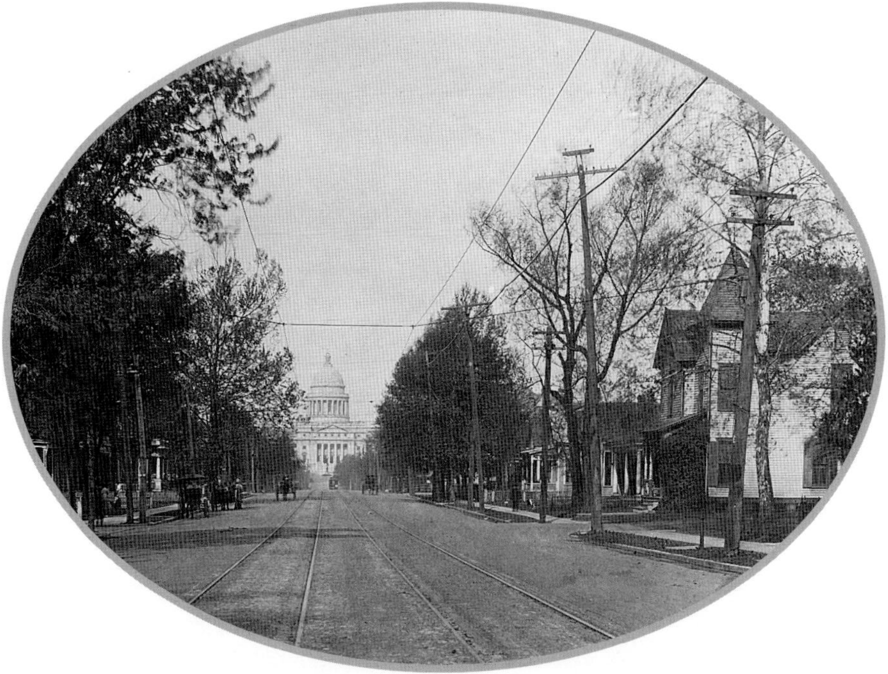

Capitol Avenue took on added significance when the State Capitol Building was built in Little Rock in 1900, on what was then the far western side of the city. Twin streetcar tracks, running in each direction, were laid along the stately boulevard that ran between Main Street and the Capitol, shown here in the distance. Today the streetcars are gone and the grand homes have all been replaced by commercial structures. (c. 1911.)

In June 1911, 19-year-old aviator Jimmy Ward and his older partner Hugh Robinson thrilled crowds for three days with performances on the grounds of the Country Club. Thousands of Little Rock residents paid 50¢ each to watch the men's aerial feats, only eight years after the Wright brothers made the first powered flight. Some of Ward's flights lasted up to 20 minutes and reached heights of 1,600 feet, with aerobatic stunts such as figure eights. The *Arkansas Democrat's* front-page story said that "more than 100 automobile parties whizzed to the place in their speedy cars."

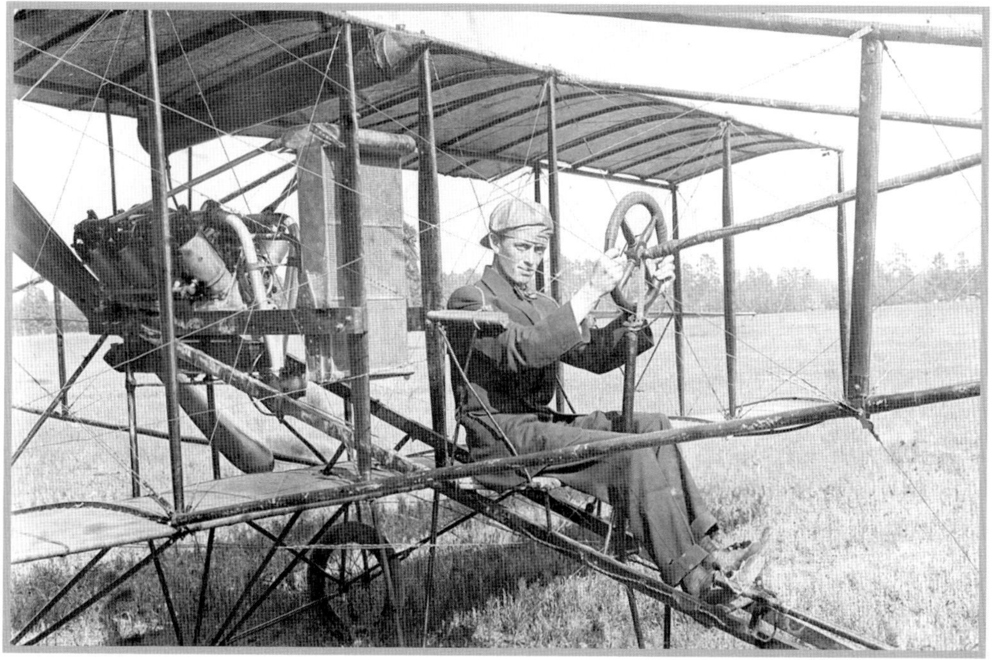

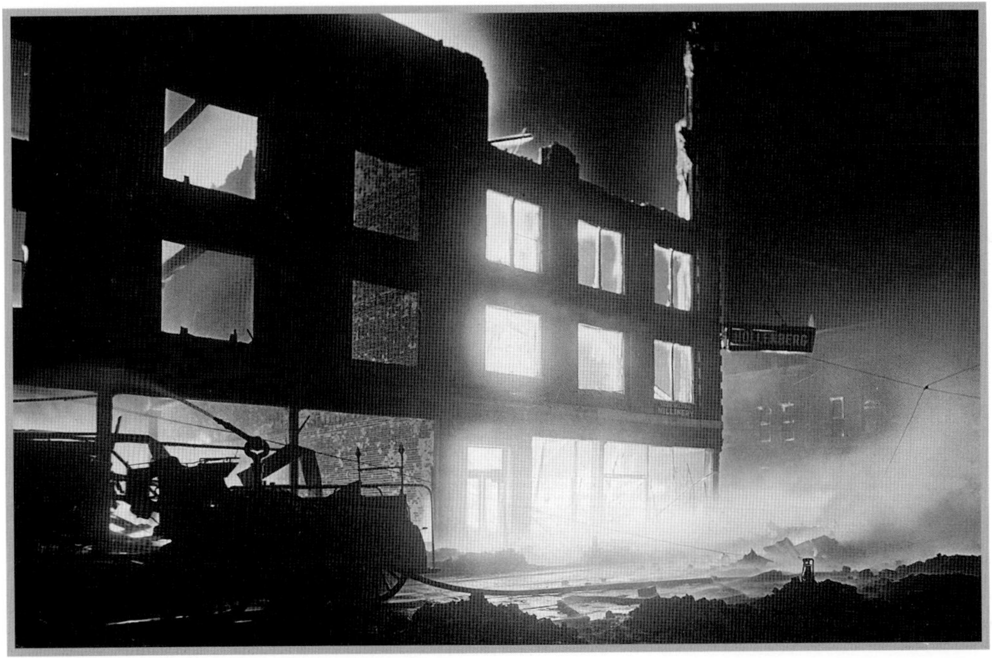

On January 2, 1911, the worst fire in Little Rock's history began on the upper floor of the Hollenberg Music Store (center), apparently from a discarded cigarette, and soon spread to the Jackson-Hanley Hardware store (left). In this picture the city's antiquated fire equipment is shown feebly shooting a weak stream of water onto the inferno. The city used this tragedy to support its appeal for upgraded firefighting equipment. The blaze lasted five hours and caused a $1 million loss.

In perhaps the most dramatic photograph of the great fire, the front of a brick store building collapses onto Main Street as spectators watch. In the distance to the right is the Masonic Temple and to the left is the State National Bank Building. Almost the entire block of Main between Sixth and Seventh Streets was lost. Crowds filled the surrounding downtown streets in the subfreezing weather, but when the flames reached the Martin Arms Company, which housed ammunition and fireworks, the *Arkansas Gazette* reported that "the din resembled the rattling of field guns," and the crowds had to dodge a barrage of fireballs unleashed when a large supply of roman candles was ignited.

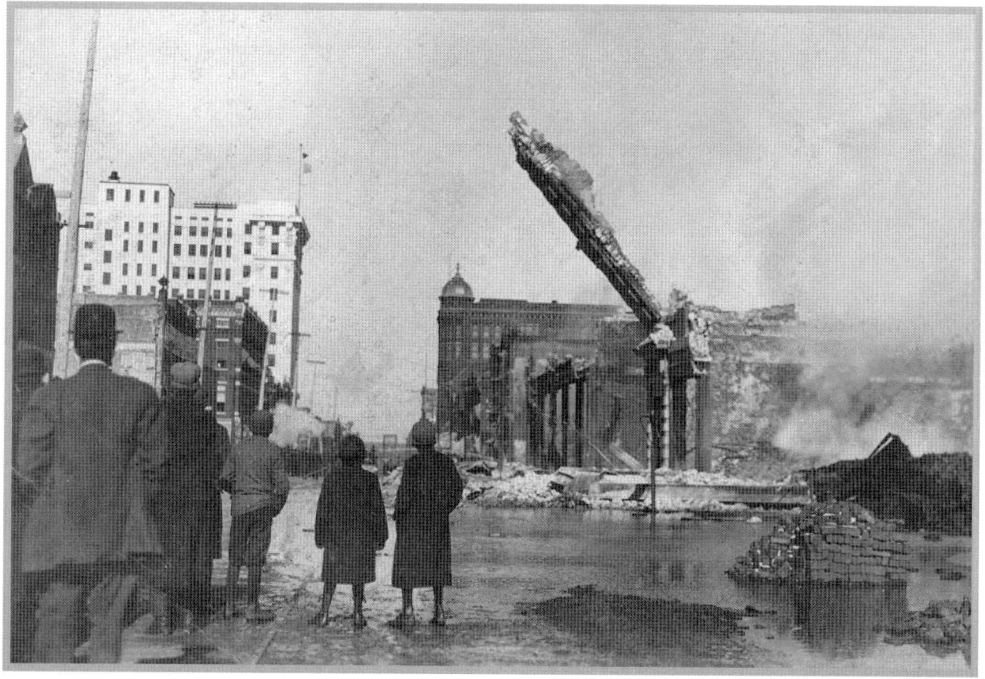

In May 1911 Little Rock hosted the 50th annual reunion of the United Confederate Veterans. The meeting brought 11,000 former soldiers to town, along with thousands of other visitors including a reunion of the "Negro body servants" who cared for the Confederate officers and did camp chores during the war.

OPPOSITE: At certain times the public was admitted to Camp Shaver to visit the veterans. Over three days the men were fed 54,000 meals, from provisions including 16,000 loaves of bread, 8,000 pounds of steak, 3,000 pounds of roast, 110 cases of eggs, and 1,700 pounds of coffee.

Camp Schaver
U.C.V. Reunion
Little Rock Ark.
May 15-18-11

In 1908 this new city hall building, designed by Charles Thompson, was erected at the corner of Markham and Broadway. In 1956 the city's electorate voted by postcard to remove the dome, visible in this 1914 photograph, rather than expend the funds to repair it. Today the building still serves, but with a flat roof.

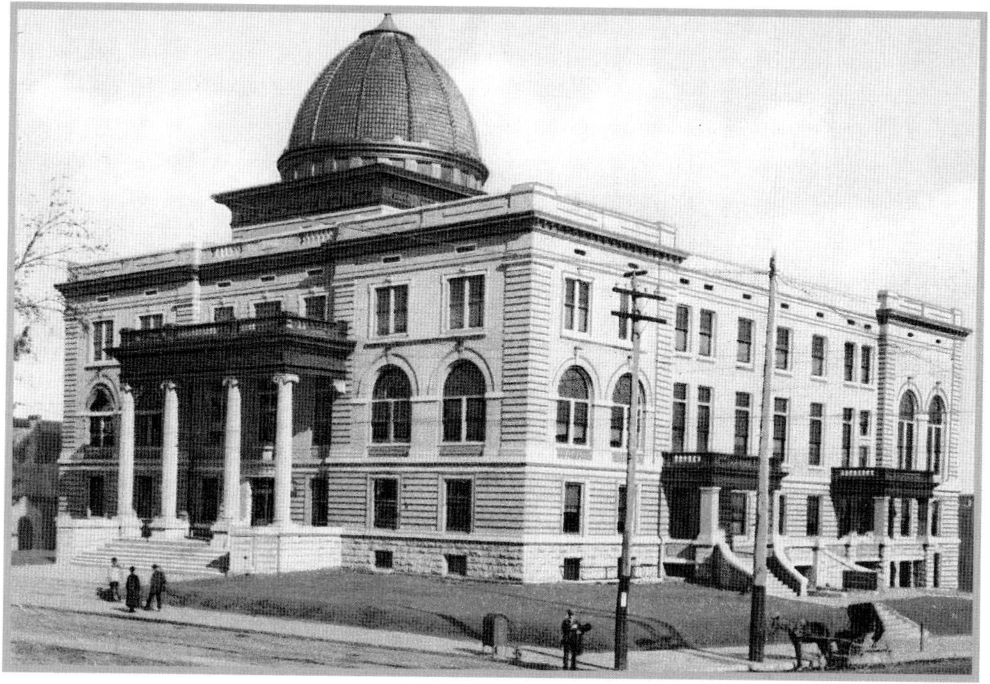

City Market and Arcade Building, Little Rock, Ark.

Little Rock's first shopping mall was the City Market and Arcade Building, which opened on Louisiana Street across from St. Andrew's Cathedral in 1914 at a cost of $137,000. It had a vaulted roof that arched over a long hallway of shops including greengrocers, jewelers, candy shops, bathhouses, cobblers, and merchants offering fine meats and groceries. Apartments on the second floor were often rented to stock company actors who worked for the nearby Kempner Theater. The building was demolished in 1959.

Proving that 24-hour pharmacies are not a recent development in American cities, this 1915 photograph of Snodgrass and Brace's Rexall Drug Store in the 100 block of Main Street shows a pennant hanging from the ceiling reading, "Open all night—hasn't closed in 14 years." The store opened in 1899 at 100 Main, and by 1931 had 10 different departments. The business even manufactured some products, including "Brain Storm Capsules" for dogs. Fire destroyed the building in the 1930s.

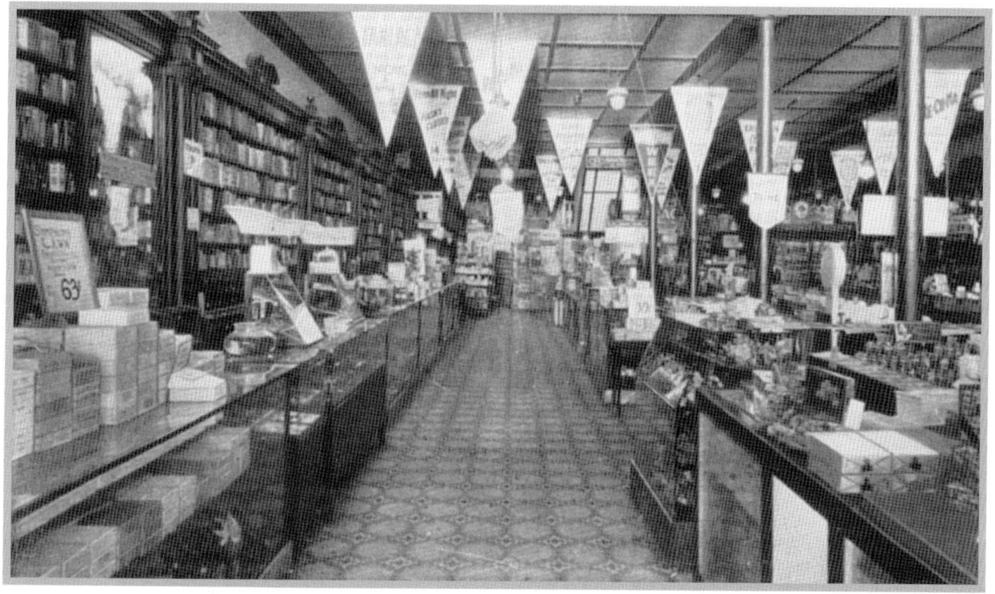

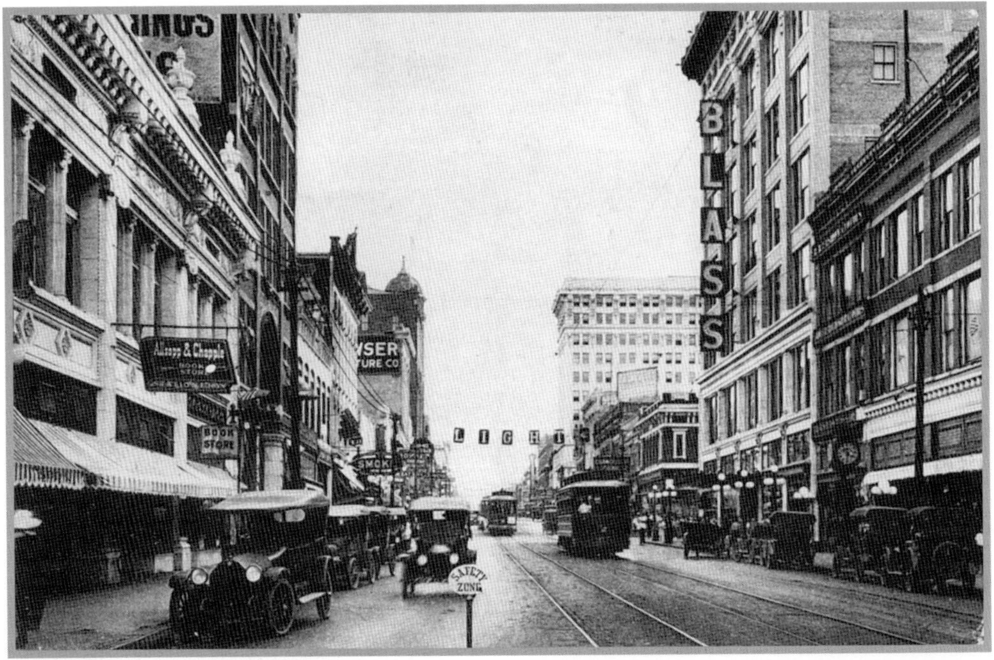

Allsopp & Chapple
BOOK STORE
BLASS
LIGHT
SMOK
SAFETY ZONE

This 1918 photograph shows the view looking south from the 400 block of Main Street. Of particular note is the "safety zone" sign in the foreground, apparently intended to keep pedestrians out of the path of the busy streetcars.

Likely the grandest of Little Rock's early movie theaters, the Palace was featuring *The Trap*, a silent western story, in this 1920 photograph. The theater faced Capitol Avenue just behind the Jewish Synagogue. Today the 30-story Regions Bank building occupies the site.

OPPOSITE: The Savoy Theater sat in the 500 block of Main Street. On the Saturday in 1918 when this photograph was taken, the silent film *The Prisoner of Zenda* starring James Hackett was showing. In addition to the various posters promoting the movie, framed portraits of some of the actors are on display at left.

90

JAMES K. HACKETT
THE PRISONER OF ZENDA
JAMES K. HACKETT
THE PRISONER OF ZENDA
TODAY
SAVOY THEATRE LITTLE ROCK. ARK.

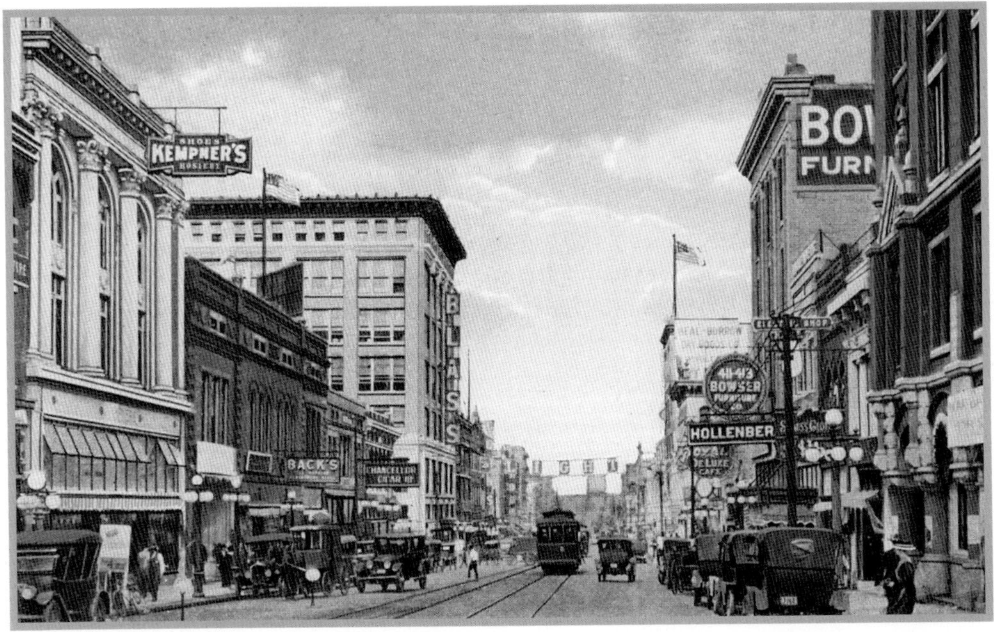
SHOES
KEMPNER'S
BACK'S
BLASS
BOW
FURN
41-43
BOWSER
HOLLENBER

Looking north down Main Street from Fifth c. 1920, such notable businesses as Kempner's (left), Blass Department Store (center), and Bowser's Furniture (right) are visible. The Hollenberg Music Store, relocated after the fire of 1911, stands beside the DeLuxe Cafe.

In 1919, three Little Rock businessmen led by William Drake set up shop on East Seventeenth Street to manufacture the automobile they named "the Climber," one of which is shown in this c. 1922 photograph. The company advertised its cars in the *Arkansas Gazette* as having "essential goodness and permanent value," with prices between $1,200 and $2,400. The Climber Motor Corporation built and sold around 200 vehicles before going bankrupt in 1924. Banks refused to finance the rather expensive vehicles.

95

The 11-story Lafayette Hotel opened at Sixth and Louisiana Streets in 1925 with 300 fireproof rooms including baths and circulating ice water. Closed from 1933 to 1941, the hotel closed for good in 1973. It gained new life in the 1980s with its conversion to an office building and is now largely occupied by various state agencies.

Opposite: The Hotel Marion's greatest claim was its grand lobby, with features designed by architect George Mann, who also played a key role in designing the new state capitol. Famous guests included Eleanor Roosevelt, Harry Truman, Douglas MacArthur, Will Rogers, Helen Keller, and Charles Lindbergh. Boarded up throughout the 1970s, it was demolished in 1980 to make way for the Peabody Hotel and the city's new convention center. (c. 1910.)

11146. Lobby Hotel Marion, Little Rock, Ark.

The Union Trust Company building was erected in 1929, in a distinguished Art Deco architectural style. In later years the business became Union National Bank, which moved from this building to a new high-rise structure in 1969. This very serviceable and architecturally significant building was torn down in 1978 to make way for a parking lot.

99

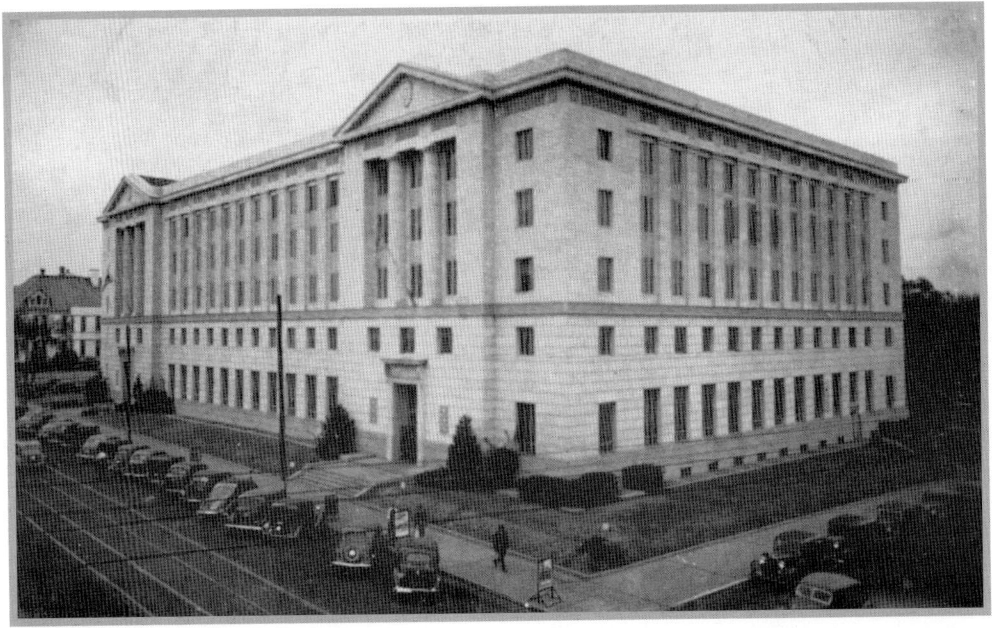

In the depths of the Depression, this impressive new post office was completed at Capitol Avenue and Gaines Streets in 1932. The Peabody School (far left) was torn down in the 1950s to make way for a new federal building, when the government outgrew the building seen in this 1930s view. Today the building is used entirely for federal courts.

"I AIN'T MAD AT NOBODY," proclaimed the sign over the door to Young's Tire and Service Company at 801 Broadway in this *c.* 1941 photograph. The sign was directed toward those who purchased gasoline on credit during the Depression and never paid off their accounts. Now that times were good again, Young wanted paying customers and was willing to forgive past unpaid debts.

ROYAL CROWN
ROYAL CROWN
YOUNG'S
Tire & Service Co.
SERVICE
SINCLAIR
H-C
GASOLINE
CENTURY
SINCLAIR
LEADED
GASOLINE
MOTOR OIL
KENDALL
QUAKER STATE
MOTOR OIL
OIL-PLATE

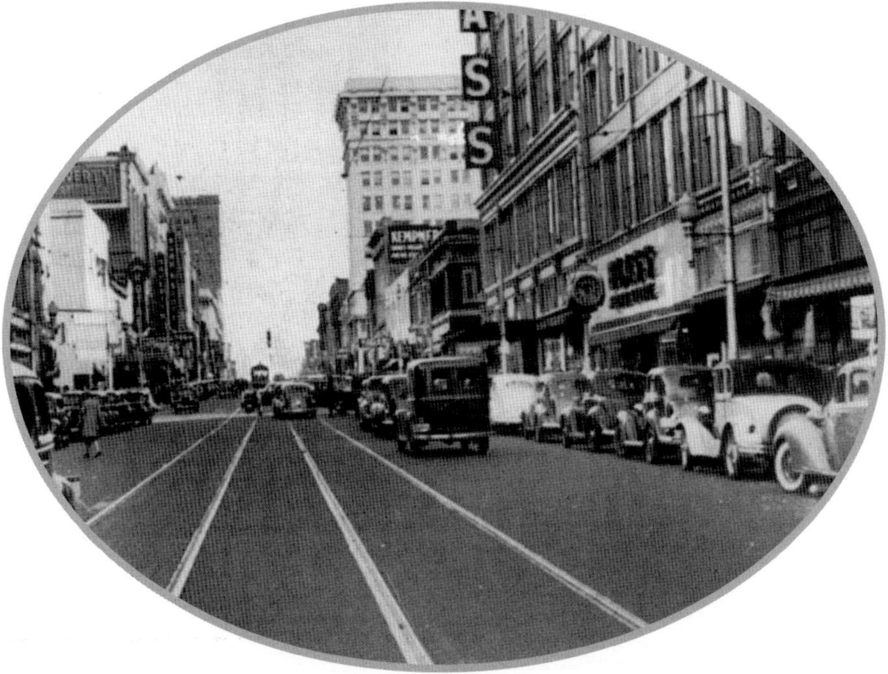

Little Rock's Main Street remained the retail center of the county in the 1940s—the first suburban shopping center was still more than a decade away. In this c. 1941 view, a single streetcar can be seen in the distance. Its days were numbered; in 1947, a fleet of buses replaced all of the streetcars.

While troops trained across the river at Camp Robinson in 1943, local businessmen stopped outside the offices of the *Arkansas Gazette* to study a posted map tracking the progress of the war effort in Europe.

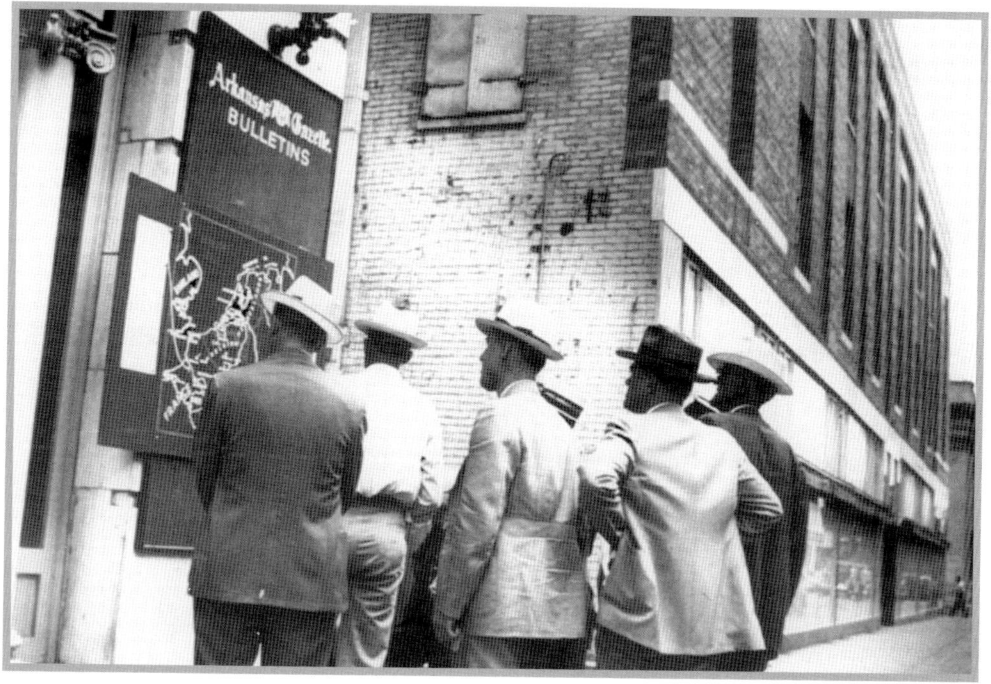
Arkansas Gazette
BULLETINS

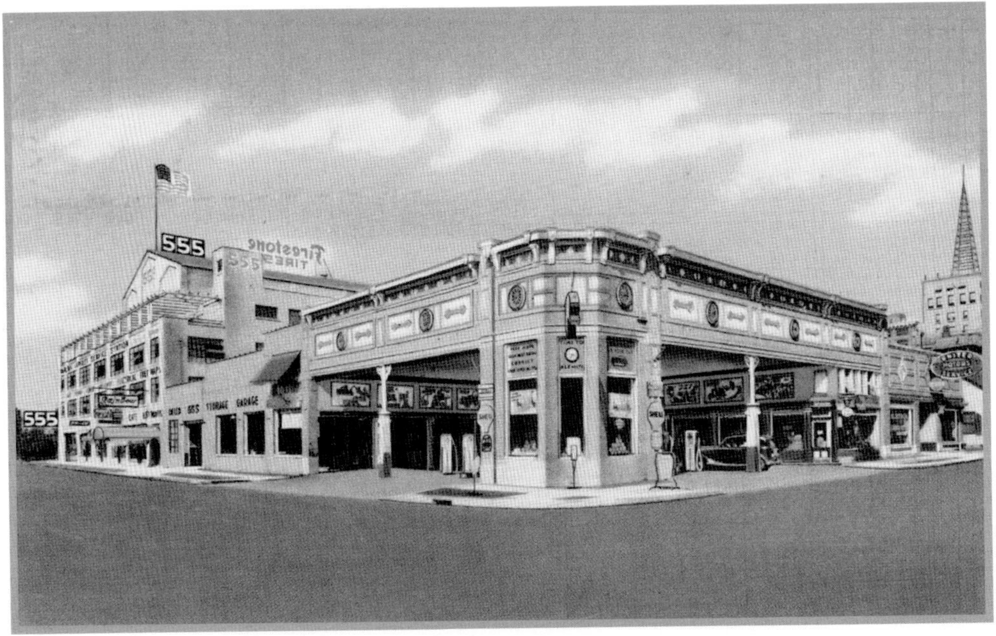
555
555
STORAGE GARAGE

The 555, Inc. Auto Center, at the intersection of four major highways, billed itself as "The World's Largest Service Station." Since it took up an entire block at Third and Broadway Streets, the claim may have been factual. The building stood diagonally opposite from the Robinson Auditorium. In this c. 1945 view, the flagpole and the prominent "Firestone Tires" sign marked the location of the Rainbow Garden, a popular dance club, on the top floor of the building. Billed as "The South's Most Beautiful Ballroom" and later known as the "Nut Club," the nightclub in the mid-1940s promised the largest dance floor and the best music in the city. Patrons were drawn by special events such as Friday dance contests, Saturday "Whoopee Nite," and Tuesday bargain night (women got in free, while men paid 40¢ to see the floor show). The building was razed around 1960 to make way for an insurance office.

Dr. John Brinkley operated his hospital at Twentieth and Schiller Streets and promoted his sometimes unorthodox healing methods on national radio. Among his procedures was one reported to cure impotence through a transplant of goat testicles. In local usage, it was said that if someone was in a hurry they might be moving "like a goat past Brinkley hospital." After more than a decade of controversy and investigation, the federal government put Dr. Brinkley out of business. (c. 1945.)

BRINKLEY
HOSPITAL
BRINKLEY
HOSPITAL
Brinkley Hospital
20th and Schiller Ave.
Little Rock, Ark.

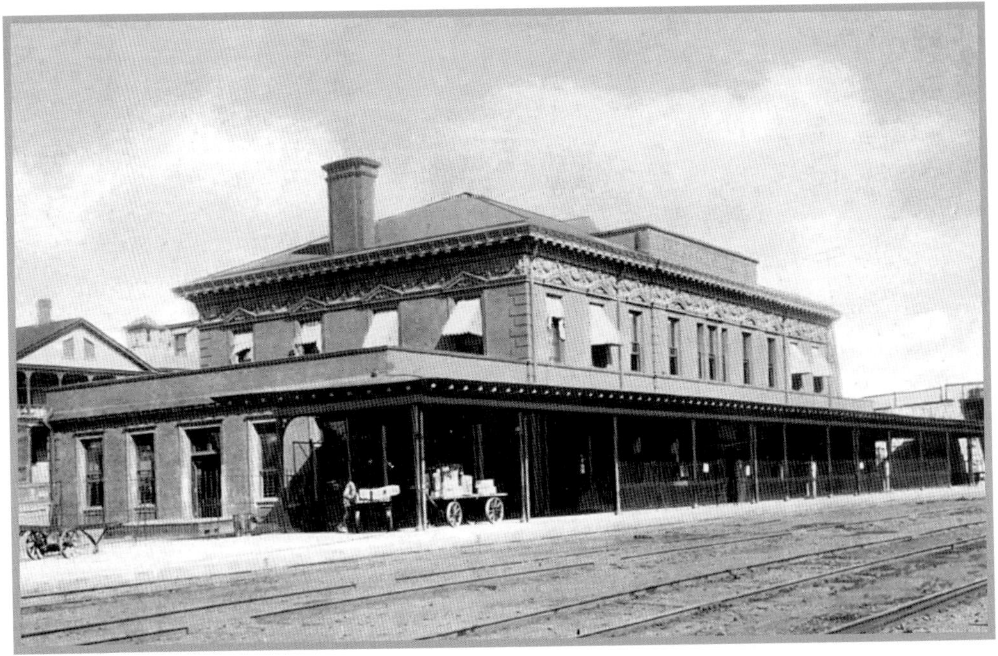

Little Rock was home to two railroad stations. Photographed c. 1910, this station on East Third Street was erected in 1899 and belonged to the Rock Island Line. When built, the station belonged to the Choctaw, Oklahoma, and Gulf Railroads, but was sold to the Rock Island in 1902. The station served passengers until the 1950s, then sat idle and decaying for several years before it was restored in the 1980s for use as a restaurant and nightclub and now serves as part of the Clinton Presidential Library and Museum Complex.

In the late 1940s, War Memorial Stadium was erected on the developing western edge of the city. In decades to follow, the stadium (with seating for more than 40,000 fans, seen here c. 1950) hosted many football games played by the University of Arkansas Razorbacks. The first stadium sell-out came in 1954, when the Razorbacks thrilled their fans by defeating Ole Miss 6-0 with a spectacular 66-yard touchdown pass.

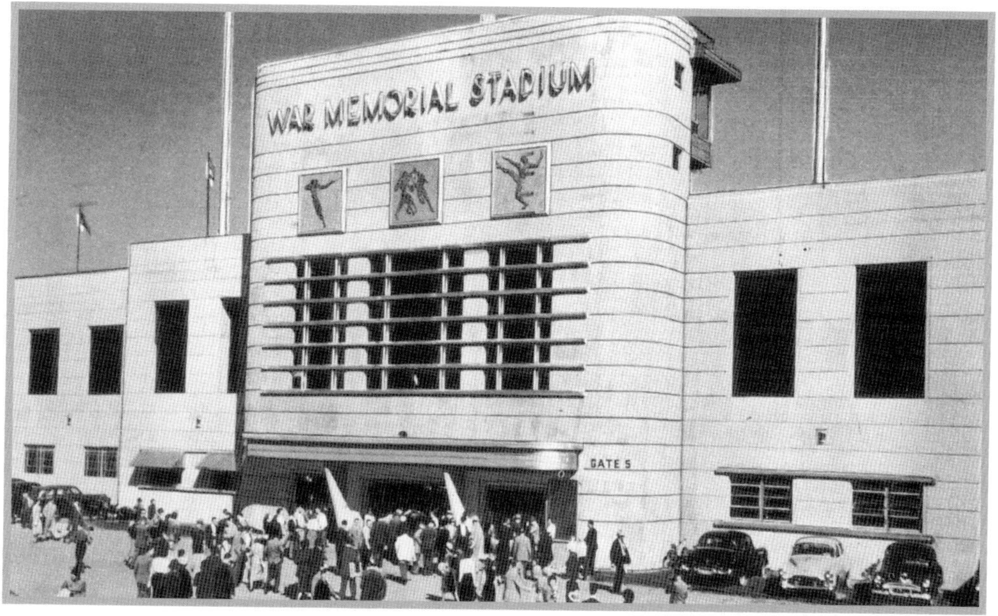
WAR MEMORIAL STADIUM
GATE 5

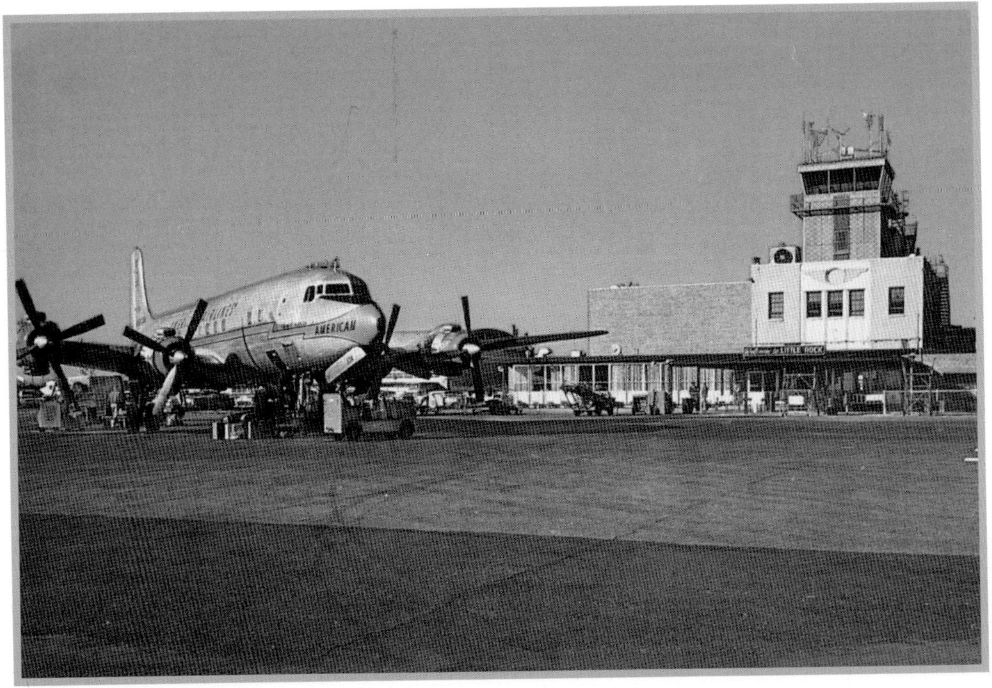
AMERICAN
LITTLE ROCK

American Airlines began flying into Little Rock in the 1940s, giving the city a major boost. Today the expanded facility known as Little Rock National Airport is served by almost all the nation's major airlines. (c. 1950.)

Support for the Confederacy continued long after most of the veterans of the 1911 reunion went on to their final camping ground. Pictured here in 1950 in front of Summerfield's Ice Cream on South Main were three adorned members of the Little Rock Chapter of the United Daughters of the Confederacy.

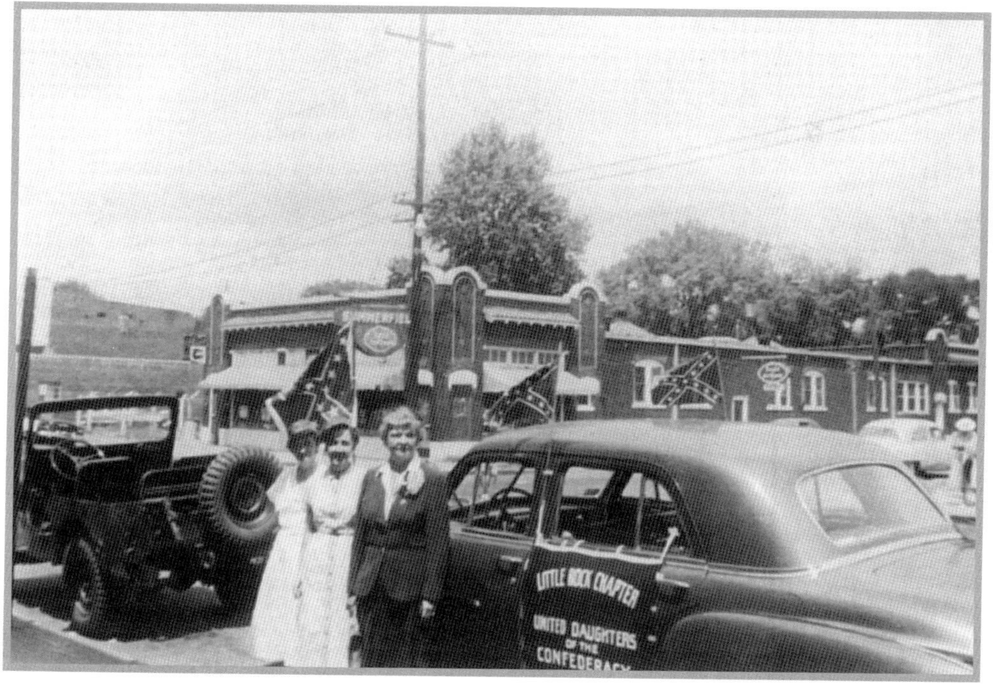
LITTLE ROCK CHAPTER
UNITED DAUGHTERS
OF THE

Pfeifer's Department Store sent this 1953 card to those on its customer list, advertising the sale of Palm Beach suits; slacks were $10.95, and a two-pants suit sold for $40.90. Over the years, postcard advertising has given way to newspaper and television promotion.

OPPOSITE: The intersection of Sixth and Main Streets is seen in this 1950s photograph from the post-streetcar era, with a bus visible in the distant right. On the left is McClellan's "five and dime"—today a parking lot. Across the street on the right is Pfiefer's Home Center and Standard Furniture. Pfiefer's was long ago absorbed into Dillard's Department Stores, and its building is the present home of the Arkansas Repertory Theater.

121

The Lido Inn was at the corner of Main Street and Roosevelt Road. A 1950s ad described the restaurant as "One of Little Rock's smartest eating places." No trace of the building remains today. With the coming of the interstate and the western expansion of the city, the Lido and other businesses along Roosevelt Road faded away.

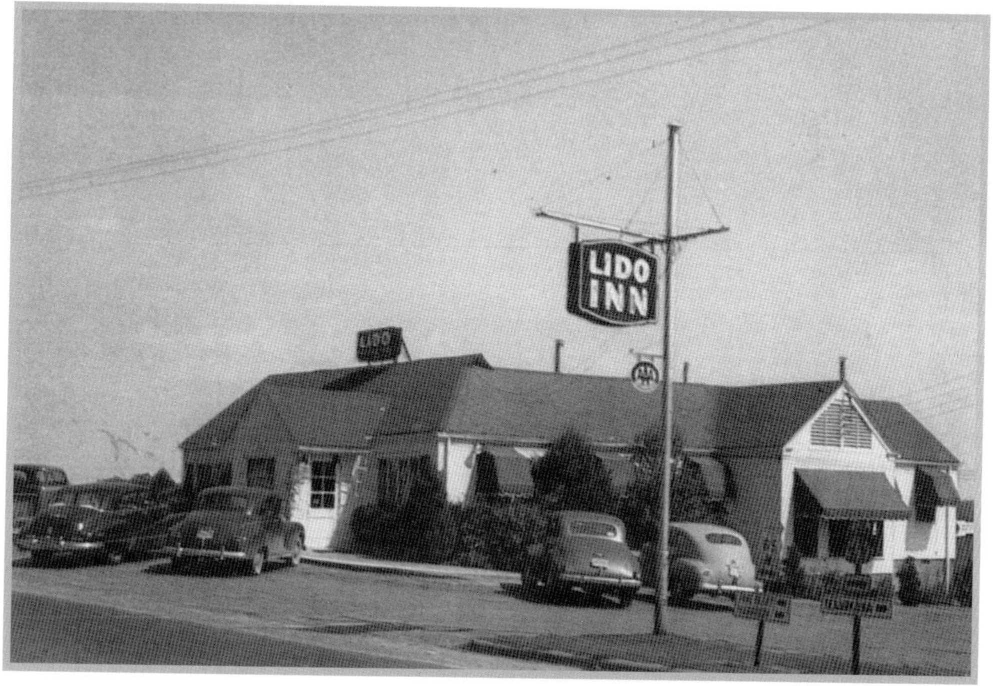
LIDO
INN
LIDO

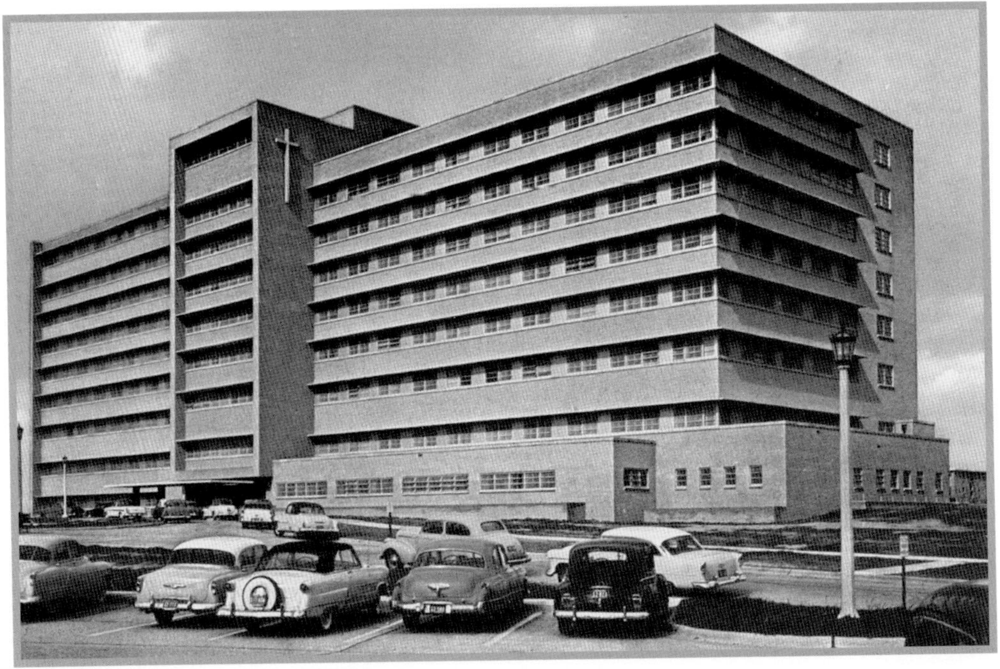

In 1954, St. Vincent Infirmary relocated from its High Street location to this modern nine-story hospital building at Markham and Hayes Streets (later University Avenue). The hospital continued to expand; with the acquisition of adjacent Columbia Doctors Hospital in 1997, St. Vincent's was poised to become the largest hospital system in the state. This represents significant progress, considering the facility started with six nuns coming to Little Rock in 1888.

In September 1957, Gov. Orval Faubus mobilized the Arkansas National Guard to prevent nine black students from integrating Little Rock's Central High School. After court hearings and front-page confrontations, President Eisenhower federalized the National Guard and finally sent 1,200 battle-equipped troops to enforce the desegregation rulings. This rare "occupied Arkansas" postcard was printed during this tumultuous time.

OPPOSITE: To the surprise of many, Orval E. Faubus, a teacher from the Ozark Mountains and small-town newspaper publisher, defeated Gov. Francis Cherry in the 1954 election. Faubus was elected six times and served for 12 years.

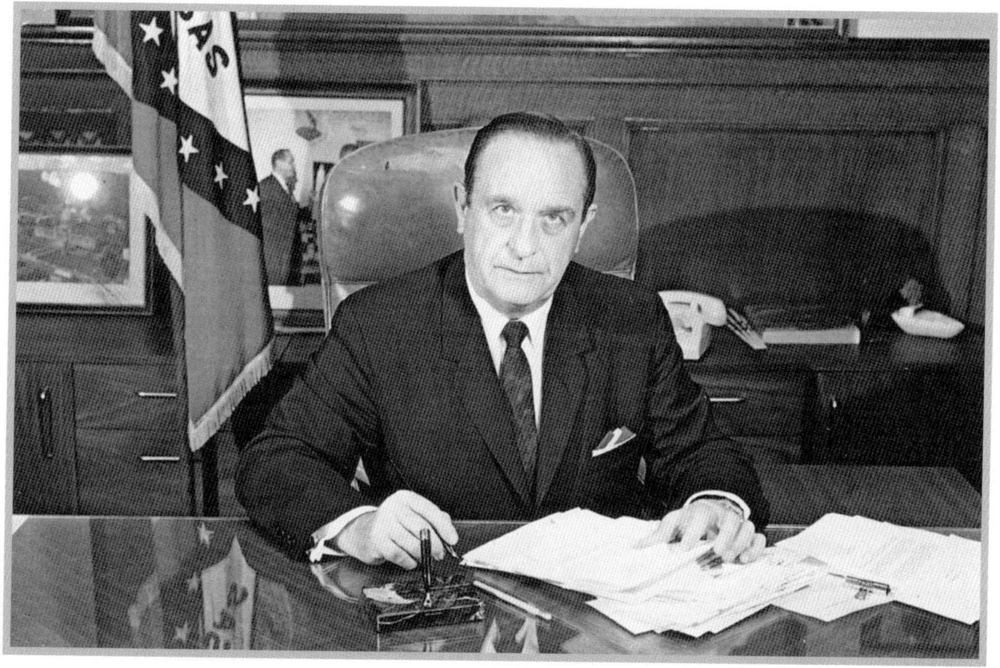

Arcadia Publishing is the leading local history publisher in the United States. With more than 3,000 titles in print and hundreds of new titles released every year, Arcadia has extensive specialized experience chronicling the history of communities and celebrating America's hidden stories, bringing to life people, places, and events from the past. To discover the history of other communities across the nation, please visit:

www.arcadiapublishing.com

Customized search tools allow you to find regional history books about the town where you grew up, the cities where your friends and relatives live, the town where your parents met, or even that retirement spot you've been dreaming of. The Arcadia website also provides history lovers with exclusive deals, advanced notice of new titles, e-mail alerts of author events, and much more.